Contents

How to Use This Book

The goal of *Reading Comprehension* is to increase the learners' proficiency in reading comprehension skills at the kindergarten level. The subject matter featured in these activities has been chosen based on curriculum used in schools nationwide. The activities and skills follow a sampling of the National Council of Teachers of English (NCTE) standards, with a focus on science and social studies topics. These activities have been designed to capture the learners' interests by presenting material in a fun and exciting way.

Reading Comprehension is organized into six sections: Words and Pictures, Following Directions, Making Predictions, Reading for Understanding, Responding to Text, and Word Meanings. Each section focuses on an important aspect of reading comprehension, offering easy-to-understand skill definitions and activity directions.

Words and Pictures

The activities in this section will help early readers attach meanings to words they hear and pictures they see. Learners will get practice reading a chart, using picture clues, and matching words to pictures.

Following Directions

In this section, learners are given opportunities to listen to and read directions in several different ways. Skills that focus on following directions using concepts such as *on* and *under* are featured. Activities in this section also focus on following one- and two-step directions as well following the steps in a process.

✏️ Making Predictions

In this section, learners will draw conclusions and make judgments about what they hear or read in a story. Learners will receive practice with using picture clues and context clues to predict a word in a sentence. An activity designed to teach learners to interpret the visual details in a picture is also included.

✏️ Reading for Understanding

In this section, learners will receive instruction in how to use a story map to help them organize information they have read. They will also learn to answer *who, what,* and *where* questions about a story to gain understanding of the content. Activities in this section also focus on sequencing pictures and drawing a picture to illustrate the meaning of a story.

✏️ Responding to Text

In this section, early learners will form an understanding of how words and pictures can create different feelings. Also featured are activities that help learners discriminate between things that are real and things that are make-believe. Learners will also benefit from activities that focus on understanding the main idea of a story and using context clues.

✏️ Word Meanings

The final section provides activities that connect words with pictures and helps learners understand the meanings of words. Learners will receive practice in identifying words in the following categories: action words, rhyming words, words with opposite meanings, and describing words.

Name _____

Snack Chart

Picture clues help us understand the meanings of words.

▭▭▷ **Directions: This chart shows the foods that children in Mrs. Brown's class ate for a snack. Use the chart to answer the questions. Write the answers on the lines.**

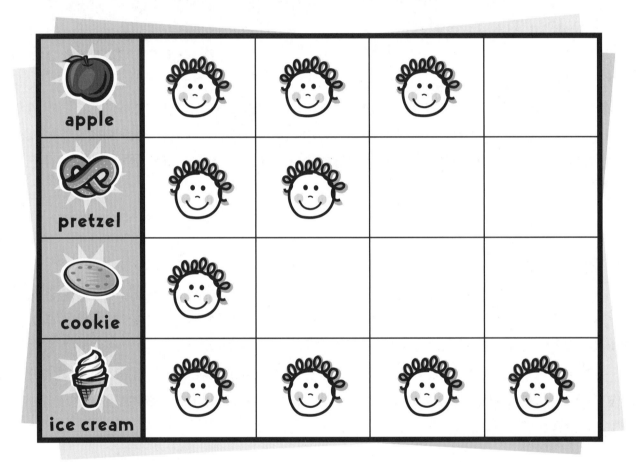

1. Did more children eat pretzels or ice cream?

_____

2. Which snack did the fewest children eat?

_____

3. Which snack did the most children eat?

_____

4

Name _____

Read and Do

Directions give the reader a specific purpose for reading.

✏️▷ **Directions: Read and follow the directions.**

1. Color the book blue.

2. Color the bear brown.

3. Color the fish orange.

✏️▷ **Directions: Read and follow the directions.**

  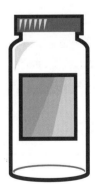

4. Put an X on the cat.

5. Circle the jar.

6. Draw a line under the ball.

5

Name _____

Tell a Story

We can make predictions by looking at a picture and guessing what will happen next.

Directions: Look at the picture. Make up a story about what will happen next. Write the story on the lines below.

_____

_____

_____

Name _____

The Birthday Party

Telling what happens in a story helps us understand what we read.

✏️ **Directions: Read the story. Write the answers to the questions on the lines.**

Jim and Pat go to a **birthday party**. They play **games**.

They eat **cake**. They open **gifts**.

1. Where do Jim and Pat go?

_____

2. What do they eat?

_____

3. What do they open at the party?

_____

7

Name _____

Bedtime

Words and pictures help us understand the story and answer questions about what we read.

Directions: Listen to the story. Circle the picture that answers each question.

> I get ready for bed. I wash my face and hands. I brush my teeth. I get into bed. My dad reads a book to me.

1. What do I do to get ready for bed?

2. What will I do after I get into bed?

8

Name _____

Action Words

Some words describe an action a person is doing.

✏️▷ **Directions: Look at the picture. Read the sentence. Circle the word that completes the sentence.**

1. The boy is _____.
   running   swimming

2. The girl is _____.
   riding   reading

Opposites

Some words have opposite meanings.

✏️▷ **Directions: Color the picture that shows the opposite meaning of the underlined word in each sentence.**

3. The dog is <u>inside</u> the house.

4. The elephant is <u>big</u>.

9

Teaching Tips...

**For *Words and Pictures*
(pp. 11–15)**

Background

• Understanding the connection between words and pictures helps learners grasp the meanings of new words. Teaching words within the familiar context of the learners' life experiences enhances their listening and reading comprehension.

Homework Helper

• Have the learner find a magazine picture and make up a sentence about it. Write the sentence as they dictate to you. Read the sentence with the learner and point out words that name things in their picture.

Research-based Activity

• Have learners choose a category such as food, animals, or kinds of transportation. Help them find picture-words in this category in a picture dictionary. Ask learners to draw a picture of each thing and write the word below it. Have learners share the results of their research with a partner or small group.

Test Prep

• Learners at this level are introduced to activities that will prepare them for the testing format they will encounter on standardized tests beginning in the higher elementary grades. The test preparation skills covered in this section include activities such as: interpreting charts and following written directions.

Different Audiences

• To adapt this section for a special needs learner, focus on their listening comprehension skills first. Provide additional practice by repeating the same skill several times in similar hands-on activities.

Name _____

Hot or Cold?

Pictures can help us think about how something feels.

Directions: Use a red crayon to circle the pictures that show things that feel hot. Use a blue crayon to circle the pictures that show things that feel cold.

Challenge: Name some other things that feel hot or cold.

11

Name _____

We Like to Play

Pictures on a chart can help us find information.

> **Directions:** Listen to the story. Read the chart to find out how many children like to ride bikes and how many children like to throw balls. Answer the questions.

The children like to play. They like to have fun. They like to ride bikes. They like to throw balls.

| bike | boy | boy | girl | girl | girl |
| ball | boy | boy | boy | boy | girl |

1. How many boys like to ride bikes? _____

2. How many girls like to ride bikes? _____

3. How many girls like to throw balls? _____

4. How many boys like to throw balls? _____

Challenge: Draw a picture of what you like to play.

12

© Rosen School Supply•Brain Builders Reading Comprehension•K•RSS

Name _____

The Toy Store

Matching words to pictures helps us remember the word.

Directions: Read the story. Follow the directions.

I go to the toy store. I see a red ball. I see a blue car.
I see a green frog. I see a purple book.

Color the **ball** red. 	Color the **book** purple. 
Color the **frog** green. 	Color the **car** blue. 

Challenge: Think of a color that was not named in the story. Draw a picture of a toy with that color.

Name _____

Silly Sentences

The beginning sounds in words can give us clues about words we don't know.

Directions: All the words in each sentence have the same beginning sound. Circle the word that completes each sentence.

1. Bob buys big

_____.

   cars   **books**

2. Many monkeys make

_____.

   music   **hats**

3. Cats can _____.

   jump   **color**

4. Tim Turtle takes two

_____.

   cars   **toys**

Challenge: Think of a sentence in which every word begins with the same sound as the first letter of your name.

14

Name _____

Skill Check—Words and Pictures

✏️▷ Directions: Look at the picture. Listen to the story. Circle the answers to the questions. Color the picture.

We went to the circus. We saw a clown with big feet. We saw two horses jumping over a gate. We saw three white bears dancing. We saw seals with balls on their noses. We had fun!

1. What were the horses doing?
   running   **jumping**

2. What color were the bears?
   white   **brown**

3. What did the seals have on their noses?
   hats   **balls**

TEACHING TIPS

Background

• Following directions is an important skill that learners will use throughout their lives. Teaching learners to follow multistep directions is a way to provide them with the language concepts and listening skills they need to understand what they read.

Homework Helper

• On separate slips of paper, write a series of five directions for a scavenger hunt in the learner's home. (Example: Go to the kitchen. Find the red cup.) Guide the learner with following the directions. Ask them to recall which direction was first, second, third, and so on.

Research-based Activity

• Help learners make up directions for a game they want to play. Simplify the directions to five steps. Have the learner use the directions to teach another person how to play the game. Discuss the end results.

Test Prep

• Learners at this level are introduced to activities that will prepare them for the testing format they will encounter on standardized tests in higher elementary grades. The test preparation skills covered in this section include: using context clues and following directions.

Different Audiences

• When working with an ESL learner, ask them to identify picture-words first in their own language and then in English. Next, have them listen to and follow one direction at a time. Have them repeat each direction in English.

16

Name _____

Where Is It?

We can use pictures to help us read and understand sentences that tell us where something is.

➤ **Directions: Look at the pictures. Read each sentence. Circle the correct answer.**

1. The dog is _____ the table.

    over   **under**

2. The book is _____ the table.

    on   **under**

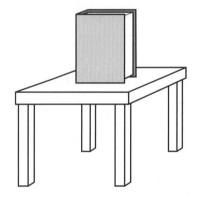

3. The cat is _____ the tree.

    over   **next to**

Challenge: Can you follow these directions? Put a book: on your head, next to you, under you.

17

Name _____

Clown Colors

Every day we follow directions that we hear.

Directions: Listen to the directions. Color the picture.

1. Color the clown's hat blue.

2. Color the clown's shoes purple.

3. Color the clown's suit green.

4. Color the clown's nose red.

5. Color the clown's hair orange.

6. Color the clown's balloons yellow.

Challenge: Look around the room. Name something that matches each color you used for the clown picture.

Name _____

Match Up

We can find a picture by listening to the directions that tell about it.

Directions: Listen to each set of directions. Draw a line from each sentence to the matching picture.

1. Find the picture that shows the boy playing ball.

2. Find the picture that shows the cat in the tree.

3. Find the picture that shows the dog in the yard.

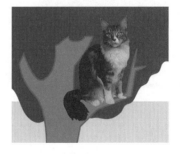

Challenge: Read a storybook. Point to the pictures in the book that the words are describing.

Name _____

Sound Search

We can follow two steps to complete a task.

Directions: Listen to the directions. Color the pictures.

ball   bear   ten

table   turtle   box

1. Color the pictures red that begin with the same sound as the word **bell**.

2. Color the pictures green that begin with the same sound as the word **top**.

Challenge: How many other things can you name that begin with the sounds of **b** and **t**?

Name _____

Skill Check—Following Directions

✏️ **Directions: Look at the pictures. Follow the directions.**

1. Put a circle around the cat on the table.

2. Draw a line under the ball.

✏️ **Directions: Listen to the words. Color the picture that begins with the same sound.**

3. map   mom   mouse

4. boy   bat   box

Teaching Tips...

Background

• At this level, pictures are often used to help learners make predictions about what a story will be about or what will happen next. Activities based on making judgments and interpreting pictures help learners build a foundation for using higher-level reading comprehension skills.

Homework Helper

• Show the learner a picture of people in a setting. Tell a story about the picture. Stop right before the ending. Ask the learner to tell how they think the story should end.

Research-based Activity

• Show learners how to use educational software that focuses on making predictions about a story they listen to on the computer. Ask parent volunteers and older students to instruct early learners on the basics of computer use and to provide help as needed.

Test Prep

• Learners at this level are introduced to activities that will prepare them for the formats they will encounter on standardized tests beginning in the higher elementary grades. The test preparation skills covered in this section include: answering multiple-choice questions and writing a story.

Different Audiences

• When instructing an accelerated learner, challenge them to write a story about additional pictures similar to those on pages 25 and 26. As a follow-up activity, have learners choose a book to read and make up a new ending for it.

22

Name _____

What Do You Think?

When we read, we use both pictures and words to help us understand what is happening.

> **Directions:** Read each set of sentences. Choose an action word from the box below that completes the sentence.

reading	playing	sleeping

1. The  is in . He is _____.

2. The  is holding a . She is _____.

3. The  have a . They are _____.

Challenge: Look at the pictures in a book. Tell what you think the story is about.

23

Name _____

What Will Happen Next?

We can predict an answer to a question by using information we already know.

Directions: Listen to each question. Look at the picture. Circle the answer.

1. How will the girl get to the top?

   jump   **climb**

2. It is snowing. What else will the girl put on?

   a hat   **a swimsuit**

3. What will the boy do with the ball?

   read it   **throw it**

Challenge: Read a story. Think of a different ending to the story.

Name _____

The Park

We can use the ideas we get from looking at a picture to make up a story.

Directions: Look at the picture. Write a story about the picture on the lines below.

_____

_____

_____

Challenge: Look at a picture from a magazine or newspaper. Make up a story about it.

Name _____

Pictures Can Tell a Story

Looking at a picture can help us think of what might happen next.

✏️ **Directions: Write a sentence about each picture that tells what will happen next.**

1. _____

_____

_____

_____

2. _____

_____

_____

_____

Challenge: Look at a picture in a book. Tell what you think will happen before reading the next part of the story.

Name _____

Skill Check—Making Predictions

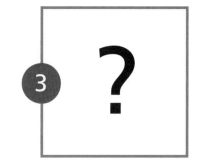

1. Which picture comes next?

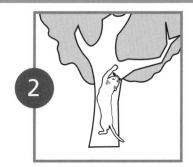

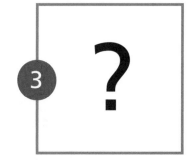

2. Which picture comes next?

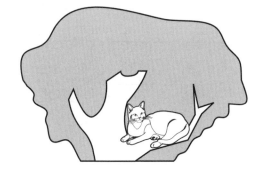

27

Teaching Tips...

Background

• It is important to teach early learners that words in sentences have meaning. Reading simple stories and answering questions about them helps learners focus on who the story is about, what they are doing, when and where the story takes place, and how it ends.

Homework Helper

• Ask the learner to read a simple story similar to the one on page 29. Assist them with making a story map that asks the questions **who, what, when, where,** and **how**. Guide the learner with answering each question based on the information from the story.

Research-based Activity

• Show learners how to use educational software that focuses on skills such as: identifying the main idea, answering questions about a story, and sequencing events. Ask parent volunteers and older students to instruct early learners on the basics of computer use and to provide help as needed.

Test Prep

• Learners at this level are introduced to activities that will prepare them for the formats they will encounter on standardized tests beginning in higher elementary grades. The test preparation skills covered in this section include following directions and answering questions.

Different Audiences

• When instructing a special needs learner, have them listen as you read aloud the stories on pages 29 and 32. Next, have them read the story with you. Have learners draw pictures in response to the questions.

Name _____

Finding Food

Writing down the facts of a story can help us remember what the story is about.

Directions: Read the story. Complete the story map by drawing pictures or writing words.

The fish is in the water. It is happy. It likes to swim. It finds food. It eats the food.

Who is the story about?

Where is the fish?

What does the fish like to do?

What happens in the story?

How does the story end?

Challenge: Use the story map to tell someone the story.

Name _____

A Helper

Drawing a picture about what we read helps us understand the story.

Directions: Listen to the story. Draw a picture of the person the story is about.

This person is a helper. She helps us cross the street. She helps us if we are lost. She helps us if we are afraid. She helps us follow the rules.

Challenge: Draw a picture of another helper in your community.

Name _____

Growing a Flower

We can use pictures to show the order of how things happen.

Directions: Look at the pictures. Write the numbers 1, 2, and 3 next to the pictures to show the order in which they happen.

Challenge: Plant a flower seed in a pot and watch it grow. Draw pictures to show how it looks as it grows.

Name _____

The Zoo

Good readers think about the answers to the following questions when they are reading: **Who** *is the story about?* **What** *are they doing?* **Where** *is the story happening?*

✏️ **Directions: Read the story. Answer the questions.**

Don and Mary go to the  . They see a  ,

a , and an  . Don and Mary have fun.

1. Who is the story about?

_____

2. Where do Don and Mary go?

_____

3. What do Don and Mary see?

_____

Challenge: Draw a picture of an animal you would like to see at the zoo.

32

Name _____

Skill Check—Reading for Understanding

Cookies

 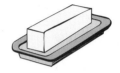

I help my mom make **cookies**. First we mix **butter**,

eggs, and other things in a **bowl**. Next we bake the

cookies in the **oven**. Then we eat the **cookies**.

1. What do we do first?

   eat the cookies   **mix**

2. What do we do last?

   eat the cookies   **bake the cookies**

33

Teaching Tips...

TEACHING TIPS

Background

• Once learners have developed an understanding of what they are reading, they will also have feelings and opinions about it. When we ask learners to tell how a story made them feel or to make a judgment about a character or event, they are responding to the text.

Homework Helper

• Provide a nonfiction or fiction story. Ask the learner to listen to the story or read it with you. Guide them with writing a summary of the story. Discuss how a person's interests and opinions may affect the kinds of stories they choose to read.

Research-based activity

• Provide opportunities for learners to read both a nonfiction and a fiction book. Ask learners to vote on the book they liked the best and tell why. Chart the results on a simple pictograph or bar graph. Have learners discuss the results.

Test Prep

• Learners at this level are introduced to activities that will prepare them for the format they will encounter on standardized tests beginning in higher elementary grades. The test preparation skills covered in this section provide practice with multiple-choice questions.

Different Audiences

• When working with an ESL learner, provide opportunities for them to read the text in the activities in their own language and in English. Allow learners to give their answers to questions orally in both languages.

34

Name _____

Happy or Sad?

The words we read can make us feel happy or sad.

 Directions: Read each sentence. How does it make you feel? Color the 😊 if it makes you feel happy. Color the 🙁 if it makes you feel sad.

1. Ron plays with a puppy.

2. Tom hurt his arm.

3. Jan is at the zoo.

Challenge: Make up a sentence that makes you feel happy or sad.

Name _____

The Five Senses

The words we read give us clues that can help us answer a question.

Directions: Listen to each description. Circle the picture that answers each question.

1. I **smell** something cooking. What part of my body do I use to **smell** things?

2. I **see** a rainbow in the sky. What part of my body do I use to **see** things?

3. I **hear** the doorbell ring. What part of my body do I use to **hear** things?

4. I **feel** the cold snow. What part of my body do I use to **feel** things?

5. I eat an orange. What part of my body do I use to **taste** things?

Challenge: Draw a picture of yourself that shows the five body parts in the activity above.

36

Name _____

The Library

The main idea of the story is what the story is about.

Directions: Listen to the story. Write the answer to each question.

Jill and Sam want to read at home. They go to the library. They each ask for two books. Then they check out books to take home.

1. Who is this story about?

   _____

   _____

2. Why do Jill and Sam go

   to the library?

   _____

   _____

Challenge: Read a story. Tell a friend what the story is about.

Name _____

Is It Real?

Words and pictures can help us decide if something we are reading about is real or make-believe.

Directions: Read each sentence. Color the picture that shows something that is real.

1. This is a cat.

2. The horse can jump.

3. The bus can go.

Challenge: Name three things that are real and three things that are make-believe.

38

Name _____

Skill Check—Responding to Text

▭▷ Directions: Read the story. Write the answers to the questions.

The Farm

Tim goes to the farm. He sees cows and pigs. He feeds the pigs. He helps the farmer.

1. Who is the story about? _____

2. Where does the story take place? _____

3. What does Tim see? _____

▭▷ Directions: Circle yes or no to answer the question.

4. Can a bird fly?   **yes   no**

5. Can a man run?   **yes   no**

6. Can a cat read a book?   **yes   no**

Teaching Tips...

TEACHING TIPS

Background
- Giving learners opportunities to expand their vocabulary and increase their understanding of word meanings helps them strengthen their reading comprehension skills.

Homework Helper
- Ask the learner to make up three sentences using action words from page 41 and describing words from page 44. Have them dictate these sentences to an adult and draw a picture illustrating each one.

Research-based Activity
- Show learners how to use educational software that focuses on rhyming words, opposites, verbs, and adjectives. Ask parent volunteers and older students to instruct early learners on the basics of computer use and to provide help as needed.

Test Prep
- Learners at this level are introduced to activities that will prepare them for the format they will encounter on standardized tests beginning in higher elementary grades. The test preparation skills covered in this section include: practice with multiple-choice questions and sentence completion.

Different Audiences
- When working with accelerated learners, challenge them to use two words from each activity (pages 41–44) to write a story about a chosen topic. Have learners read their stories to a friend.

Name _____

Action Words

We use action words to tell what someone is doing.

Directions: Look at each picture. Circle the word that tells what the person is doing.

walking

riding

walking

jumping

reading

painting

climbing

running

Challenge: Name five actions you like to do.

41

Name _____

Rhyme Time

Listening for the rhyming sounds in words can help us read new words.

Directions: Read each rhyming sentence. Circle the picture of the word that completes each sentence. Write the word on the line.

1. The frog is on the _____.

apple   log

2. The wig is on the _____.

pig   dog

3. The cat sat on the _____.

hat   pin

Challenge: Draw pictures of the rhyming word pairs above. Write the words under the pictures.

Name _____

Opposites

Sometimes words have opposite meanings.

✏️➤ **Directions: Read each sentence. Circle the word that has the opposite meaning of each underlined word.**

1. A frog is <u>little</u>.

   A horse is _____.

   big   **small**

Ann   Tom

2. Ann is <u>tall</u>.

   Tom is _____.

   tall   **short**

3. The boy is <u>happy</u>.

   The girl is _____.

   short   **sad**

Challenge: Can you name three other pairs of words with opposite meanings?

Name _____

The Yellow Cat

Words that tell how something looks or feels help us form pictures in our minds.

Directions: Listen to the poem. Circle the words that describe the cat. Draw a picture of what you see in your mind.

I once had a yellow cat.
He was big, he was fat.

My yellow cat had soft, soft fur
He liked to sit and gently purr.

My yellow cat would run and play.
Then he would sleep the whole next day!

Challenge: Listen to some poems or nursery rhymes without looking at the pictures first. Compare the pictures in your mind to the pictures in the book.

Name _____

Skill Check—Word Meanings

✏️ **Directions:** Look at each picture. Circle the rhyming sentence that matches it.

1. A bug is on a rock.

   A bug is on a rug.

2. A man drives a van.

   A man drives a car.

The Apple

✏️ **Directions:** Read the story. Draw a picture of what the story describes.

I see an apple. It is big. It is red. It has a hole in it. It has a small, brown worm in the hole.

Answer Key

p. 4
1) ice cream
2) cookie
3) ice cream

p. 5
1) The book should be colored blue.
2) The bear should be colored brown.
3) The fish should be colored orange.
4) The cat should have an X on it.
5) The jar should be circled.
6) There should be a line drawn under the ball.

p. 6
Learners' answers will vary.

p. 7
1) Jim and Pat go to a birthday party.
2) They eat cake.
3) They open gifts.

p. 8
1) Picture of girl brushing her teeth should be circled.
2) Picture of dad reading to girl in bed should be circled.

p. 9
1) The boy is <u>swimming</u>.
2) The girl is <u>riding</u>.
3) The picture of the dog outside the house should be colored.
4) The picture of the smaller elephant should be colored.

p. 11
The following pictures should have a red circle around them:
• pot on the stove
• cup with steam coming from it
• the Sun
The following pictures should have a blue circle around them:
• snowflakes
• ice cream cone
• snowman

p. 12
1) Two boys like to ride bikes.
2) Three girls like to ride bikes.
3) One girl likes to throw a ball.
4) Four boys like to throw balls.

p. 13
• The ball should be colored red.
• The book should be colored purple.
• The frog should be colored green.
• The car should be colored blue.

p. 14
1) Bob buys big <u>books</u>.
2) Many monkeys make <u>music</u>.
3) Cats can <u>color</u>.
4) Tim Turtle takes two <u>toys</u>.

p. 15
1) The horses were jumping.
2) The bears were white.
3) The seals had balls on their noses.

p. 17
1) The dog is <u>under</u> the table.
2) The book is <u>on</u> the table.
3) The cat is <u>next to</u> the tree.

p. 18
1) The clown's hat should be colored blue.
2) The clown's shoes should be colored purple.

46

3) The clown's suit should be colored green.
4) The clown's nose should be colored red.
5) The clown's hair should be colored orange.
6) The clown's balloons should be colored yellow.

p. 19
1) A line should be drawn to the picture showing the boy playing ball.
2) A line should be drawn to the picture showing the cat sitting in the tree.
3) A line should be drawn to the picture showing the dog in the yard.

p. 20
1) The pictures that should be colored red are as follows: ball, bear, box.
2) The pictures that should be colored green are as follows: 10, table, turtle.

p. 21
1) The cat should be circled.
2) The ball should be underlined.
3) The moon should be colored.
4) The bed should be colored.

p. 23
1) He is sleeping.
2) She is reading.
3) They are playing.

p. 24
1) climb
2) a hat
3) throw it

p. 25
Learners' answers will vary.

p. 26
Learners' answers will vary.

p. 27
1) The picture of the girl holding a cone with no ice cream should be circled.
2) The picture of the cat at the top of the tree should be circled.

p. 29
1) Who is the story about? —The story is about a fish.
2) Where is the fish? — The fish is in the water.
3) What does the fish like to do? —The fish likes to swim.
4) What happens in the story? — The fish finds food.
5) How does the story end? — The fish eats the food.

p. 30
The picture should be of a school crossing guard.

p. 31
• There should be a number 2 written next to the top picture.
• There should be a number 3 written next to the middle picture.
• There should be a number 1 written next to the bottom picture.

p. 32
1) The story is about Don and Mary.
2) They go to the zoo.

3) They see a tiger,
   a bear, and
   an elephant.

p. 33
1) mix
2) eat the cookies

p. 35
1) The happy face should
   be colored.
2) The sad face should
   be colored.
3) The happy face should
   be colored.

p. 36
1) The nose should
   be circled.
2) The eyes should
   be circled.
3) The ears should
   be circled.
4) The hand should
   be circled.
5) The mouth should
   be circled.

p. 37
1) The story is about
   Jill and Sam.
2) Jill and Sam go
   to the library to
   get books.

p. 38
1) The first picture of
   the cat should be
   colored.
2) The first picture of
   the horse should be
   colored.
3) The second picture
   of the bus should be
   colored.

p. 39
1) The story is
   about Tim.
2) The story takes place
   on the farm.
3) Tim sees cows
   and pigs.
4) yes
5) yes
6) no

p. 41
1) riding
2) jumping
3) reading
4) climbing

p. 42
1) The frog is on the log.
2) The wig is on the pig.
3) The cat sat on the hat.

p. 43
1) A horse is big.
2) Tom is short.
3) The girl is sad.

p. 44
Learners' pictures
will vary.

p. 45
1. A bug is on a rug.
2. A man drives a van.
3. A picture of a big red
   apple. There should
   be a small, brown
   worm coming out of
   a hole in the apple.